LEADERSHIP 101

Inspirational Quotes & Insights for Leaders

101

JOHN C. MAXWELL

HB
HONOR
BOOKS

Leadership 101 — Inspirational Quotes and
  Insights for Leaders

6th Printing
Over 135,000 in Print

ISBN 1-56292-077-4
Copyright © 1994 by John C. Maxwell
1530 Jamacha Road, Suite D
El Cajon, California 92019

Published by Honor Books
P.O. Box 55388
Tulsa, Oklahoma 74155

Introduction

Leaders are readers! Even thousands who don't read widely, read wisely. They clip out articles and file quotes for future use. For thirty years this has been my practice. Often I have been asked to share the quotes I have collected with others. This book is my attempt to fulfill this request on the subject of leadership. Long ago I learned that if you want to quote like a leader you must note like a leader. Here is the material, start filing.

John Maxwell

Leadership is influence.

John Maxwell

▼ ▼ ▼

Nothing so conclusively proves a man's ability to lead others as what he does from day to day to lead himself.

Thomas J. Watson

Whatever you do, do it with all your might. Work at it, early and late, in season and out of season, not leaving a stone unturned, and never deferring for a single hour that which can be done just as well now.

P.T. Barnum

Leadership is not a right — it's a responsibility.

John Maxwell

▼ ▼ ▼

Real leaders are ordinary people with extraordinary determination.

Leaders who win the respect of others are the ones who deliver more than they promise, not the ones who promise more than they can deliver.

Mark A. Clement

Character is power.

Booker T. Washington

▼ ▼ ▼

The will to succeed is important, but what's more important is the will to prepare.

Bobby Knight

I studied the lives of great men and famous women, and I found that the men and women who got to the top were those who did the jobs they had in hand, with everything they had of energy and enthusiasm.

Harry S. Truman

True leadership must be for the benefit of the followers, not the enrichment of the leaders.

▼ ▼ ▼

Failing organizations are usually over-managed and under-led.

Warren G. Bennis

Use power to help people. For we are given power not to advance our own purposes nor to make a great show in the world, nor a name. There is but one just use of power and it is to serve people.

George Bush

Failure can be divided into those who thought and never did and into those who did and never thought.

Reverend W.A. Nance

▼ ▼ ▼

To avoid criticism, do nothing, say nothing, be nothing.

Elbert Hubbard

Leaders must be close enough to relate to others, but far enough ahead to motivate them.

John Maxwell

Leadership is the capacity to translate vision into reality.

Warren G. Bennis

▼ ▼ ▼

You manage things; you lead people.

Grace Murray Hopper
Admiral, U.S. Navy (retired)

A man must be big enough to admit his mistakes, smart enough to profit from them, and strong enough to correct them.

One of the tests of leadership is the ability to recognize a problem before it becomes an emergency.

Arnold Glasow

▼ ▼ ▼

I don't know the key to success, but the key to failure is trying to please everybody.

Bill Cosby

You are the same today that
you are going to be in five years
from now except for two things:
the people with whom you associate
and the books you read.

Charles "Tremendous" Jones

The key to successful leadership today is influence, not authority.

Kenneth Blanchard

▼   ▼   ▼

No matter what size the bottle, the cream always came to the top.

Charles Wilson
President, GE

A big man is one who makes us feel bigger when we are with him.

A ship in a harbor is safe but that is not what ships were built for.

▼ ▼ ▼

The only place success comes before work is in the dictionary.

Donald Kendall
Chairman, Pepsi Co.

You never conquer a mountain. Mountains can't be conquered; you conquer yourself — your hopes, your fears.

Jim Whitaker
1st American To Reach the Summit of Mt. Everest

He who never walks except
where he sees other men's tracks
will make no discoveries.

▼ ▼ ▼

I start with the premise that the
function of leadership is to produce
more leaders, not more followers.

Ralph Nader

Whatever I have tried to do in life, I have tried with all my heart to do it well; whatever I have devoted myself to, I have devoted myself completely; in great aims and in small I have always thoroughly been in earnest.

Charles Dickens

You can have brilliant ideas, but if you can't get them across, your ideas won't get you anywhere.

Lee Iacocca

▼ ▼ ▼

A wise leader inspires and motivates, rather than intimidating and manipulating.

Asking "who ought to be the boss" is like asking "who ought to be the tenor in the quartet?" Obviously, the man who can sing tenor.

Henry Ford

Nothing great was ever achieved without enthusiasm.

Ralph Waldo Emerson

▼ ▼ ▼

A leader is one who knows the way, goes the way, and shows the way.

John Maxwell

The best executive is the one who has sense enough to pick good men to do what he wants done, and self-restraint enough to keep from meddling with them while they do it.

Theodore Roosevelt

The single most important factor in determining the climate of an organization is the top executive.

Charles Galloway

▼ ▼ ▼

You must live with people to know their problems, and live with God in order to solve them.

P.T. Forsyth

Reportedly IBM's Tom Watson was asked if he was going to fire an employee who made a mistake that cost IBM $600,000. He said, "No, I just spent $600,000 training him. Why would I want somebody to hire his experience?"

My great concern is not whether you have failed, but whether you are content with your failure.

Abraham Lincoln

▼ ▼ ▼

Failure is the opportunity to begin again, more intelligently.

Henry Ford

The man who gets the
most satisfactory results
is not always the man with the
most brilliant single mind,
but rather the man who can
best co-ordinate the brains and
talents of his associates.

W. Alton Jones

**Show me a thoroughly satisfied man,
and I will show you a failure.**

Thomas Edison

▼ ▼ ▼

**I will have no man work for me
who has not the capacity
to become a partner.**

J.C. Penney

Here lies a man who knew how to enlist the service of better men than himself.

Andrew Carnegie's Tombstone

Luck is the residue of design.

Branch Rickey

▼ ▼ ▼

All glory comes
from daring to begin.

Eugene F. Ware

The ultimate leader is one who is willing to develop people to the point that they eventually surpass him or her in knowledge and ability.

Fred A. Manske, Jr.

Don't spend a $1.00's worth of time on a $.10 decision.

▼ ▼ ▼

Common sense in an uncommon degree is what the world calls wisdom.

Samuel Coleridge

A leader takes people where they want to go. A great leader takes people where they don't necessarily want to go, but ought to be.

Rosalynn Carter

**When rejecting the ideas
of another, make sure you reject
only the idea and not the person.**

▼ ▼ ▼

**Greatness lies not in being strong,
but in the right use of strength.**

Henry Ward Beecher

It isn't the incompetent
who destroys an organization.
The incompetent never gets
in a position to destroy it. It is
those who have achieved
something and want to rest
upon their achievements who
are forever clogging things up.

F.M. Young

Reason often makes mistakes, but conscience never does.

Josh Billings

▼ ▼ ▼

If you lay down with dogs, you'll pick up fleas.

East Texas Saying

Most people who succeed in the face of seemingly impossible conditions are people who simply don't know how to quit.

Robert Schuller

A leader is a person with a magnet in his heart and a compass in his head.

Robert Townsend

▼ ▼ ▼

To handle yourself, use your head; to handle others use your heart.

Success does not consist in never making mistakes but in never making the same one a second time.

George Bernard Shaw

The man who follows the crowd will never be followed by a crowd.

▼ ▼ ▼

Leadership only functions on the basis of trust.

John Maxwell

Nothing gives one person so much advantage over another as to remain always cool and unruffled under all circumstances.

Thomas Jefferson

All great leaders have one common spiritual gift – faith.

Elmer Towns

▼ ▼ ▼

One of the greatest gifts leaders can give others is hope.

To lead others to do right is wonderful. To do right and then lead them is more wonderful...and harder.

John Maxwell

The moment you stop learning, you stop leading.

Rick Warren

▼ ▼ ▼

When you're through improving, you're through.

A person that is successful has simply formed the habit of doing things that unsuccessful people will not do.

You will never be a leader unless you first learn to follow and be led.

Tiorio

▼ ▼ ▼

You can't build a reputation on what you're going to do.

Henry Ford

There are two ways to raise the level of leadership in your organization: (1) train them and (2) trade them.

John Maxwell

You cannot escape the responsibility of tomorrow by evading it today.

Abraham Lincoln

▼ ▼ ▼

There are no victories at bargain prices.

General Dwight D. Eisenhower

If you want to succeed you should strike out on new paths rather than travel the worn paths of accepted success.

John D. Rockefeller, Jr.

You can not push anyone up the ladder unless he is willing to climb a little.

Andrew Carnegie

▼ ▼ ▼

People support what they help create.

A good leader is a person
who takes a little more than
his share of the blame and a little
less than his share of the credit.

**The Boss depends on authority —
the Leader depends on good will.**

▼ ▼ ▼

**People do not follow programs,
but leaders who inspire them.**

John White

In reading the lives of great men,
I found that the first victory
they won was over
themselves...self-discipline
with all of them came first.

Harry S. Truman

To lead people walk behind them.

▼ ▼ ▼

Leadership is seldom official.

John Maxwell

The quickest and shortest way to crush whatever laurels you have won is for you to rest on them.

Donald P. Jones

It's what you learn after you
know it all that counts.

John Wooden

▼ ▼ ▼

The final test of a leader is that he
leaves behind in other people the
convictions and the will to carry on.

A leader is anyone who has two characteristics: first, he is going somewhere; second, he is able to persuade other people to go with him.

A leader who develops people, ADDS — a leader who develops leaders, MULTIPLIES!

John Maxwell

▼ ▼ ▼

The Boss says "go" — the Leader says "let's go."

Leadership: The art of getting someone else to do something you want done because he wants to do it.

Dwight Eisenhower

A good leader is a guy who can step on your toes without messing up your shine.

▼ ▼ ▼

We are what we repeatedly do, excellence then is not an act, but a habit.

Aristotle

A leader must be able
to concentrate under
difficult conditions – to
keep his head when all
about him are losing theirs.

Eagles don't flock — you have to find them one at a time.

H. Ross Perot

▼ ▼ ▼

A man who has to be convinced to act before he acts is not a man of action.

Georges Clemenceau

Never tell people how to do things. Tell them what to do and they will surprise you with their ingenuity.

General George S. Patton

Leadership is both something you are, and something you do.

Fred Smith

▼ ▼ ▼

The only person that can stop you from becoming what God intends for your life is YOU!

Be a yardstick of quality. Some people aren't used to an environment where excellence is expected.

Stephen Jobs

**A man who wants to lead
the orchestra must turn his
back on the crowd.**

▼ ▼ ▼

**Congealed thinking is the forerunner
of failure...make sure you are
always receptive to new ideas.**

George Crane

People and rubber bands have one thing in common: they must be stretched to be effective.

John Maxwell

Do not be afraid of going slowly, be afraid of standing still.

Eastern Proverb

▼ ▼ ▼

You cannot lead anyone else farther than you have been able to go yourself.

When you get right down
to it, one of the most important
tasks of a leader is to eliminate
his people's excuse for failure.

Robert Townsend

Be the most enthusiastic person you know.

▼ ▼ ▼

Leadership has less to do with position than it does with disposition.

John Maxwell

Ninety-five percent of achieving anything is knowing what you want and paying the price to get it.

Good leaders must first become good servants.

Robert Greenleaf

▼ ▼ ▼

Example is not the main thing in influencing others – it's the only thing.

Albert Schweitzer

Workers want a boss who
uses a baton — not a club.
They want to be led — not driven.

Ability may get you to the top — but it takes character to keep you there.

▼ ▼ ▼

A sense of responsibility is the clearest indication of mature leadership.

John Maxwell

It's OK to lend a helping hand —
the challenge is getting
people to let go of it.

Being in power is like being a lady. If you have to tell people you are, you aren't.

Margaret Thatcher

▼ ▼ ▼

Leadership is the transference of vision.

Hal Reed

There is a loftier ambition than merely to stand high in the world. It is to stoop down and lift mankind a little higher.

Henry Van Dyke

You're only as good as the people you hire.

Ray Kroc

▼ ▼ ▼

He that cannot obey cannot command.

Trust men and they will be true to you; treat them greatly and they will show themselves great.

Ralph Waldo Emerson

**I recommend you to take care
of the minutes, for the hours
will take care of themselves.**

Lord Chesterfield

▼ ▼ ▼

**An important question for leaders:
"Am I building people, or building my
dream and using people to do it?"**

John Maxwell

There are two quick ways to disaster: taking nobody's advice and taking everybody's advice.

Leadership is production, not position.

John Maxwell

▼ ▼ ▼

A wise leader resolves conflicts peaceably not forcibly.

A great leader comes along about once in a generation and great problems come along about three times a week.

One of the burdens of leadership is to be unpopular when necessary.

▼ ▼ ▼

In times like these it helps to recall that there have always been times like these.

Paul Harvey

Too many people in leadership positions prepare to answer questions that nobody is asking.

John Maxwell

**Learn to say "no" to the good
so you can say "yes" to the best.**

▼ ▼ ▼

A leader is a dealer in hope.

Napoleon Bonaparte

Leaders will not experience long-term success unless a lot of people want them to.

John Maxwell

**Outstanding leaders appeal
to the hearts of their followers,
not their minds.**

▼ ▼ ▼

**How do you recognize a leader?
His people consistently turn in
superior performances.**

Robert Townsend

No man will make a great leader who wants to do it all himself, or to get all the credit for doing it.

Andrew Carnegie

Leaders walk the talk.

John Maxwell

▼ ▼ ▼

Leadership is not a role —
it's a function.

The first and perhaps the final test of leadership is your ability to attract and keep followers.

Nothing is more common than unfulfilled potential.

Howard Hendricks

▼ ▼ ▼

Leadership means not having to be completely in harmony with everyone else.

Winston Churchill

Again and again, the impossible problem is solved when we see that the problem is only a tough decision waiting to be made.

Robert Schuller

There is no success
without a successor.

▼ ▼ ▼

Leadership is not wielding authority —
it's empowering people.

Becky Brodin

You will MAXimize your potential when you are willing to give up at any moment all that you are to receive all that you can become.

Leadership is a privilege, and with privilege comes responsibility.

▼ ▼ ▼

The nose of the bulldog has been slanted backwards so that he can breathe without letting go.

Winston Churchill

Every great institution is the lengthened shadow of a single man. His character determines the character of his organization.

Ralph Waldo Emerson

Nothing great will ever be achieved without great men, and men are great only if they are determined to be so.

Charles DeGaulle

▼ ▼ ▼

The most effective leadership is by example, not edict.

A great leader never sets himself above his followers except in carrying responsibility.

Jules Ormont

Whistler's Law: You never know who's right, but you always know who's in charge.

▼ ▼ ▼

Leadership — it takes one to know one, show one, and grow one.

John Maxwell

The most pathetic person in the world is someone who has sight but has no vision.

Helen Keller

If a man knows not what harbor he seeks, any wind is the right wind.

Seneca

▼ ▼ ▼

Attitude will make or break a leader.

John Maxwell

You do not lead by hitting people over the head — that's assault, not leadership.

Dwight D. Eisenhower

We see things not as they are, but as we are.

▼ ▼ ▼

It is only as we develop others that we permanently succeed.

Harvey S. Firestone

The highest compliment leaders can receive is the one that is given by the people who work for them.

**He who stays in the valley
shall never go over the hill.**

▼ ▼ ▼

**Successful leaders have the courage
to take action while others hesitate.**

John Maxwell

The successful leader is the one who makes the right move at the right moment with the right motive.

When the best leader's work is done the people say, "We did it ourselves."

Lao-Tsu

▼ ▼ ▼

A limit on what you will do, puts a limit on what you can do.

Leaders impress others when leaders succeed; leaders impact others when followers succeed.

John Maxwell

The leader who sells principles for popularity will soon become bankrupt.

▼ ▼ ▼

There's no gain without pain.

Benjamin Franklin

It isn't the people you fire who make your life miserable, it's the people you don't.

Harvey Mackay

Leadership is developed, not discovered.

▼ ▼ ▼

Today a reader — tomorrow a leader.

W. Fusselman

The essence of leadership is a vision you articulate clearly and forcefully on every occasion. You can't blow an uncertain trumpet.

Theodore Hesburgh

We teach what we know;
we reproduce what we are.

▼ ▼ ▼

Leadership development is a
life-time journey — not a brief trip.

John Maxwell

It is one of the most beautiful compensations of this life that no man can sincerely try to help another without helping himself.

Emerson

One test of leadership: Turn around, and see if anyone is following you.

▼ ▼ ▼

If you pay peanuts, expect to get monkeys.

It is wonderful when the people believe in their leader: but it is more wonderful when the leader believes in the people!

The first step to leadership is servanthood.

John Maxwell

▼ ▼ ▼

Trust is the glue that holds everything together. Be a leader that can be trusted!

If a leader demonstrates competency, genuine concern for others, and admirable character, people will follow.

T. Richard Chase

Proper prior planning prevents pitifully poor performance.

▼ ▼ ▼

The right man is the one who seizes the moment.

Goethe

**Leaders get out in front
and stay there by raising
the standards by which they
judge themselves – and by which
they are willing to be judged.**

Fred Smith

Have enough confidence in yourself to let the other fellow take some risk.

Robert J. Buckley

▼ ▼ ▼

There is no security on this earth — only opportunity.

The question is not "how much does this person work" but "how much does this person accomplish?"

We cannot expect people to do the right thing unless they know the right thing to do.

▼ ▼ ▼

My responsibility is to be a supervisor, not a superworker.

Fred Smith

People tend to stay motivated when they see the value to them of the things they are asked to do.

Vision is the art of seeing things invisible.

Jonathan Swift

▼ ▼ ▼

Leadership is getting people to help you when they are not obligated to do so.

I have never seen a man
who could do real work
except under the stimulus of
encouragement and enthusiasm,
and the approval of the people
for whom he is working.

Charles Schwab

All leaders will pay a price to carry out their calling.

▼ ▼ ▼

Lead, follow, or get out of the way.

Plaque on Ted Turner's Desk

Good executives never put off until tomorrow what they can get someone else to do today.

Pay now, play later;
play now, pay later.

John Maxwell

▼ ▼ ▼

Present choices determine
future consequences.

The highest purpose for faith
is not to change my circumstances
but to change me.

A desk is a dangerous place from which to watch the world.

John le Carre

▼ ▼ ▼

Even eagles need a push.

**Leadership and followership
cannot be separated.
Your followership sets the
pattern for your leadership.**

The first rule of winning: Don't beat yourself.

Football Adage

▼ ▼ ▼

Credibility is the most important possession of a leader.

John Maxwell

People tend to stay motivated when they see the importance of the things they are asked to do.

He that won't be counselled can't be helped.

Benjamin Franklin

▼ ▼ ▼

Failure to prepare is preparing to fail.

Mike Murdock

There is a great difference
between worry and concern.
A worried person sees a
problem, and a concerned
person solves a problem.

Harold Stephens

A great man is always willing to be little.

Ralph Waldo Emerson

▼ ▼ ▼

As a rule...he (or she) who has the most information will have the greatest success in life.

Disraeli

Having confidence that if you have done a little thing well, you can do a bigger thing well too.

Storey

...failing doesn't make you a failure.
Giving up, accepting your failure,
refusing to try again, does!

Richard Exley

▼ ▼ ▼

Words can show a man's wit,
but action shows his meaning.

Benjamin Franklin

A duty dodged is like a debt unpaid; it is only deferred, and we must come back and settle the account at last.

Joseph F. Newton

Dreams are the touchstones of our character.

Henry David Thoreau

▼ ▼ ▼

The most important thing about having goals is having one.

Geoffry F. Abert

Some people change jobs, mates and friends, but never think of changing themselves.

The quality of a leader is reflected in the standards they set for themselves.

Ray Kroc

▼ ▼ ▼

A leader's success is largely determined by the ability to motivate others.

Nearly all men can stand adversity, but if you want to test a man's character, give him power.

Abraham Lincoln

People buy into the leader before they buy into the vision.

John Maxwell

▼ ▼ ▼

Get the tide up and all the boats will rise.

Love and respect do not automatically accompany a position of leadership. They must be earned.

If you see a snake, just kill it. Don't appoint a committee on snakes.

H. Ross Perot

▼ ▼ ▼

The person who cannot see the ultimate becomes a slave to the immediate.

Leaders manipulate others when they move them for the leader's advantage. Leaders motivate others when they move them for everyone's advantage.

John Maxwell

People are changed, not by coercion or intimidation, but by example.

John Maxwell

▼ ▼ ▼

Few things are more powerful than a positive push.

The size of a leader is determined by the depth of his convictions, the height of his ambitions, the breadth of his vision and the reach of his love.

D.N. Jackson

Time is the most valuable thing a man can spend.

Laertius Diogenes

▼ ▼ ▼

The actions of men are the best interpreters of their thoughts.

John Locke

Lord, when I am wrong, make me willing to change; when I am right, make me easy to live with. So strengthen me that the power of my example will far exceed the authority of my rank.

Pauline H. Peters

Dr. John C. Maxwell is the Senior Pastor of the rapidly growing Skyline Wesleyan Church in Lemon Grove, California. He is also known across the world as a motivator, encourager and equipper of leaders. He has conducted leadership seminars nationally and internationally, and is the founder and director of INJOY, Inc., a leadership development company. He is the author of six books published by Thomas Nelson, Victor Books and others.

How would you like to receive a new lesson on leadership each month?

Sound great? Then join the Club...the INJOY Life Club. By becoming a member, you'll receive a new motivational tape by Dr. John C. Maxwell each month. Call **1-800-333-6506** to find out how you can join the INJOY Life Club.

INJOY is a non-denominational Christian leadership institute founded in 1984 by Dr. John C. Maxwell. INJOY is committed to increasing the leadership effectiveness of people in ministry, business, and the family. INJOY offers a wide variety of training seminars, books, videos, and audio cassettes designed to increase your ability to influence and lead others. For more information concerning John C. Maxwell or INJOY write or call:

INJOY
1530 Jamacha Road, Suite D
El Cajon, California 92019
1-800-333-6506